# CULTURE
in North and South Korea

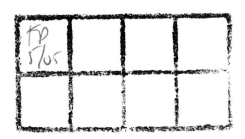

Melanie Guile

www.heinemann.co.uk/library

Visit our website to find out more information about Heinemann Library books.

To order:

 Phone 44 (0) 1865 888066

 Send a fax to 44 (0) 1865 314091

 Visit the Heinemann Bookshop at www.heinemann.co.uk/library to browse our catalogue and order online.

First published 2003 in Australia by Heinemann Library a division of Harcourt Education Australia, 18–22 Salmon Street, Port Melbourne Victoria 3207 Australia (a division of Reed International Books Australia Pty Ltd, ABN 70 001 002 357).

Series cover and text design by Stella Vassiliou
Paged by Stella Vassiliou
Edited by Carmel Heron
Production by Michelle Sweeney

Pre-press by Digital Imaging Group (DIG), Melbourne, Australia
Printed and bound in China by WKT Company Ltd.

ISBN 1 74070 130 5 (hardback)
08 07 06 05 04 03
10 9 8 7 6 5 4 3 2 1

ISBN 0 431 18131 4 (paperback)
09 08 07 06 05
10 9 8 7 6 5 4 3 2 1

British Library Cataloguing in Publication Data

Guile, Melanie.
Culture in North & South Korea.
306'.09519
A full catalogue record for this book is available from the British library.

Acknowledgements

Cover photograph of couple watching the huge lantern 'Dragon' during the Super Lantern Festival, supplied by AP/AAP/Yun Jai-hyoung, © 2002, The Associated Press.

Other photographs supplied by: AFP/AAP/Kim Jae-Hwan: p. 11; AP/AAP/ Yun Jai-hyoung, © 2002, The Associated Press: p. 12; Australian Picture Library (APL)/Corbis/© AFP: p. 8, /© ART on FILE: p. 27, /© Bohemian Nomad Picturemakers: p. 14, /© Corbis: p. 9, /© Michael Freeman: p. 17, /© Joren Gerhard: p. 13, /© Chris Lisle: pp. 7, 23, /© Massimo Mastrorillo: p. 20, /© Stephanie Maze: p. 15, /© Cardinale Stephane: p. 25 (top), /© Michael S. Yamashita: p. 19; GMM: p. 21; By kind permission of the Ho-Am Foundation: p. 23 (bottom); By kind permission of the Korean Cultural Service Library, New York: p. 26; Courtesy of the Korean National Tourist Organisation: pp. 10, 16, 28, 29; Lonely Planet Images/John Elk III: p. 18; The Nostalgia Factory: p. 25 (bottom); PhotoDisc: p. 23 (top).

Every attempt has been made to trace and acknowledge copyright. Where an attempt has been unsuccessful, the publisher would be pleased to hear from the copyright owner so any omission or error can be rectified in subsequent printings.

CONTENTS

Words that appear in bold, **like this**, are explained in the glossary on page 30.

CULTURE IN
North and South Korea

Hanging like a giant hook off the Asian mainland, the Korean **peninsula** lies between two great powers, China and Japan. The Koreans have absorbed many influences from their neighbours, yet their culture is quite distinct. Their **ancestors** were **nomads** who followed their herds through the grasslands of central Asia. The Korean language has ancient links with the languages spoken by the peoples of Turkey and Mongolia and is not related to Chinese. Around 30000 years ago these tribal people settled in the Korean peninsula and developed their own rich culture.

What is culture?

Culture is a people's way of living. It is the way in which people identify themselves as a group, separate and different from any other. Culture includes a group's spoken and written language, social customs and habits, as well as its traditions of art, craft, dance, drama, music, literature and religion.

Cult of the Kims

In North Korea, former leader Kim Il-sung and his son Kim Jong-il – the current leader – have god-like **status**. Photos of them are displayed in every home, and each citizen must wear a red badge bearing the leader's picture. Every newspaper carries several pictures of the Kims. These must never be thrown away, but cut out carefully and returned to district collection points. Anyone found using them as rubbish is arrested and sent to prison.

A nation divided

The first Korean kingdom was formed around AD 100, and remained one nation until the end of World War II in 1945, when it was divided into two countries – the **communist** north, controlled by the **USSR**, and the south, controlled by the USA. In 1950 the communists invaded the south. The Korean War that followed (1950–1953) devastated the countryside. Finally, a truce was called. But the country remained divided, and North and South Korea have developed separately for the past 50 years. So the two Koreas share common traditions and language, but daily life in each country is now very different.

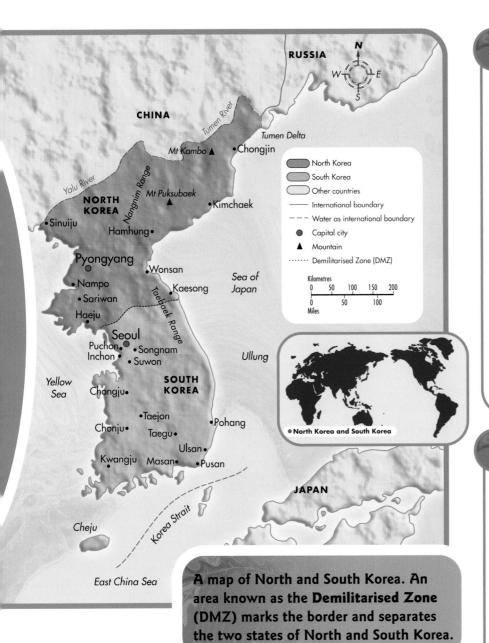

Flag of North Korea

The flag of the Democratic People's Republic of Korea (North Korea). The wide red band stands for revolutionary spirit, and the red star in the circle represents the Korean Workers' Party, which rules the country. The blue is for peace and the two white bands represent purity.

Flag of South Korea

The flag of the Republic of Korea (South Korea). The white background represents purity. The round symbol in the middle is a *Taeguk*, a Korean version of the **yin and yang**, representing balance and harmony. The three-line marks in each corner represent heaven, Earth, water and fire.

A map of North and South Korea. An area known as the **Demilitarised Zone (DMZ)** marks the border and separates the two states of North and South Korea.

In North Korea, the communist government oversees every aspect of people's lives. There is strict **censorship** and limits on travel, school and work choices. Most traditional festivals are banned and all religion is outlawed. Traditional arts and crafts are encouraged. Modern art, music, drama and literature are strictly controlled: no western influence is permitted, and North Korea must be shown in a positive light. In all artworks, the heroes must be peasants or workers, and the communist system must always be praised.

After decades of corruption and unrest, South Korea finally became a **democracy** when free elections were held in 1988. It is a modern country with a free press and a healthy economy. The arts – both modern and traditional Korean – flourish freely there.

South Korea after the Korean War

In just 50 years since the devastation of the Korean War, South Koreans have created a modern, wealthy, **democratic** country of 48 million people. It is one of the 'Asian Tigers' – countries that achieved amazing economic success after the end of World War II. This is due mainly to the huge, family-run manufacturing companies called *jaebeol* that export high-quality, South Korean-made goods worldwide, including cars, computer hardware, electrical appliances and heavy machinery. Some of the well-known *jaebeol* include Hyundai, LG (Lucky Goldstar), Daewoo and Samsung. For years, under oppressive **dictator** General Park Chung-hee (who ruled from 1961–1979), low-paid workers for these companies laboured long hours in poor conditions to build the economy. Now, in spite of an economic downturn during the late 1990s, South Koreans enjoy one of the highest standards of living in Asia.

North Korea after the Korean War

After the end of the Korean War in 1953, North Korea was locked away under the long-term **communist** dictator Kim Il-sung (who ruled from 1948–1994). His theory of the '**Juche Idea**' insisted that North Korea must not rely on any other country for goods or services, but must be totally self-sufficient. Unfortunately, the country could not produce all it needed, leading to shortages of basic food, medicines and fuel.

As a result, North Korea's 24 million people became totally **isolated** from the rest of the world. With the help of its communist neighbours, China and the **USSR**, industries were established and health clinics and schools were set up. But in the late 1980s the economy began to collapse as its main Communist backer, the USSR, broke up and withdrew support.

When Kim Il-sung's son, Kim Jong-il, took over after his father's death in 1994, North Koreans were faced with shortages, widespread poverty, strict **censorship** and economic collapse. Tension between north and south has always been severe, but, in 2000, the South Korean President at that time, Kim Dae-jung, met Kim Jong-il in the North Korean capital, P'yongyang – the first such meeting since the war. Kim Dae-jung was awarded the Nobel Peace Prize in 2000 for his efforts at **reconciliation**. His successor, Roh Moo Hyun, vows to continue on this path, but relations have soured once more and North Korea is threatening military strikes against the south.

Religions

Three religions have influenced Korean culture over the centuries: spirit worship, **Buddhism** and **Confucianism**. **Christianity** is growing strongly in South Korea where around 30 per cent of people now follow it. In the communist state of North Korea, all religion is banned.

Spirit worship

Spirit worship (called **animism** or **shamanism**) dates from prehistoric times. Today in South Korea, there are 40 000 shamans (priests) called *mudang*. These women perform **rituals**, songs and dances to drive out evil spirits and bring good fortune.

Buddhism

Buddhism is based on the life and teachings of Gautama, known as the Buddha. He was born in 563 BC in India and came to Korea around AD 300. Buddhism emphasises leading a pure, simple life in search of a state of wisdom called **enlightenment**.

Confucianism

Confucianism is based on the ideas of the ancient Chinese **scholar** Confucius. It is a set of social rules including obedience to authority, education and loyalty.

EVERYDAY LIFE
in North Korea

Since North Korea became a separate **communist** country in 1945, it has locked itself away from the rest of the world. Virtually no-one is allowed in or out, but some have escaped over the Chinese border to tell of the difficult daily life of people in North Korea.

Iron control

Everyday life is tough in North Korea. The government distributes food, housing, education and jobs, and people have no say in where they live or work. All food, clothing and household goods are given out in fixed monthly allowances. Rice, barley and vegetables are the main foods. Tea and coffee are unavailable, and people drink hot rice water. No-one may travel without permission, and to attempt to leave the country is a crime. Huge prison camps house 200 000 **political prisoners**, most of whom do not survive due to torture and the terrible conditions.

The armed forces

North Korea has a million-strong army – one of the world's largest. Officially there is no **conscription** but in reality everyone is expected to serve up to seven years. Soldiers are often used as labour on major government building projects such as roads, dams and bridges.

A woman sweeper keeps the street spotless under a statue of 'Great Leader' Kim Il-sung in North Korea's capital, P'yongyang. The city boasts an underground railway with marble floors and the world's highest fountain (150 metres tall) on the Taedong River.

Class divisions

A nationwide government survey (held 1967–1970) of citizens' loyalty to North Korea established three classes of people: the core group (28 per cent of the population) – officials of the Communist Party and their families who live **privileged** lives; the Unstable Group (45 per cent) – lower-ranked government officials and workers whose loyalty to the state is uncertain; and the Hostile Group (27 per cent) who are regarded as anti-government. This last group is used for slave labour and denied opportunities for housing, jobs and education. Only the core group are allowed to live in the capital, P'yongyang.

Family life

Around 70 per cent of people live in poverty, working long days in factories or on farms. Private homes generally have two rooms where the family sleeps on the floor and cooks in a courtyard. People work six days a week and enjoy picnics and walks in parks on Sundays. A popular outing is to view the beautiful lit-up fountains near the Mansudae Art Theatre in P'yongyang.

Shortages

A terrible **famine** gripped North Korea during 1997 and 1998. International aid organisation World Vision estimated that up to two million people starved to death. People were allowed only half a cup (100 grams) of rice per day and most were reduced to eating wild leaves and roots. International experts blamed drought, floods and poor government planning for the famine.

The policy of the **Juche Idea** (isolation from other countries) also causes shortages of petrol, household goods and medicines, which have to be imported. In 1999, all public buses outside P'yongyang were abandoned because of lack of petrol. Health care is crumbling, too. The Red Cross reported in 2001 that basic medicine and equipment were unavailable at most country health clinics.

The Red Cross distributing aid to North Korean citizens during the famine.

TRADITIONS
and customs

Vanishing cultures

Korean traditions are under threat both north and south of the **Demilitarised Zone** (DMZ) – for different reasons. In wealthy, westernised South Korea, many locals worry that ancient traditions and customs are being swamped by international and US culture. They feel that traditional values like respect, self-control and politeness are being replaced by more casual, western-style values. In North Korea, military-style **communist** control has banned most traditional customs and festivals. People now celebrate special days for workers such as Miners' Day and Labour Day rather than Buddha's Birthday. But leader Kim Jong-il shows signs of lightening up, and traditions like *Dangun* Festival, which marks the ancient founding of Korea, have quietly crept back.

Personal relationships

In Korea, well-established rules apply in social relations. The key idea of *kibun* (good, harmonious feelings between people) ensures no one is embarrassed or loses face. Open disagreement is rare and conflict is avoided. The ideas of Confucius (who lived around 500 BC) also influence life throughout Korea. The 'Five Relationships' set out rules of behaviour for master and servant, father and son, husband and wife, young and old, and friendships. Loyalty to family and respect for authority are important, and children are expected to obey their parents on matters like dating and careers.

Gender roles

In traditional Korea, women took responsibility for the home, the children and household accounts, but men made key decisions. Under **Confucian** law, women did not go to school or take paid work, and had to obey their husbands and elder sons. **Ancestor**-worship **rituals** were performed only by males, and sons cared for their parents in old age, so girl babies were often unwanted and abandoned at birth.

Children pay respects to their parents at Lunar New Year. Respect for elders is an important Korean tradition.

Women in North and South Korea

Under communism, women are regarded as equal to men, so North Korean girls are educated, work on family farms, serve in the army and are appointed jobs. Still, women are expected to be the homemakers. Shortages of food and fuel mean women and children must walk long distances to gather wild food.

South Korean women's roles have improved greatly over the past 50 years. They now receive 12 years of schooling and have paid jobs. Nevertheless, in this male-**dominated** culture, women generally have lower pay and less powerful positions. There are few female politicians or business executives. Home duties are very important and good *kimchi* (pickled cabbage) is still the sign of a good housewife.

Taekwondo

Korea's national sport is *taekwondo*, which means 'the art of kicking and punching'. It developed in Korea over 2000 years ago as mental and physical training exercises (martial arts) for soldiers. *Taekwondo* is similar to karate but emphasises rapid, athletic kicking with the feet. Mental strengths are also important and include courage, obedience and self-control.

Male culture

Male dominance is expressed in many aspects of modern life in Korea. Korean men identify themselves as heroic soldiers, famous for their **endurance** and battle cunning. Admiral Yi Sun-sin is a national hero in the north and south. In 1592 he defeated a huge Japanese invading navy, sinking 500 of their ships using his new invention – iron-clad 'turtle ships'. Korean men are also protective of their women and frown upon the common practice of western men marrying Korean girls. Male-dominated outdoor sports are very popular in South Korea, including wilderness hiking, mountain biking, skiing and the national sport, *taekwondo*.

Throughout Korea, most families have just two children. Boys are valued more than girls because they are expected to look after their parents in later life (girls look after their in-laws), they continue the family lineage and financially contribute more to the family. In South Korea, 116 males are born for every 100 females, which means there is a severe shortage of girls. This is because many parents decide to end the pregnancy if they know the **fetus** is female. It is now illegal in South Korea for doctors to tell parents the sex of their unborn child. North Korea does not have this problem.

Education

Education is extremely important in Korea. Twelve years of schooling are **compulsory** in South Korea and parents and teachers push the pupils very hard. Most children attend after-school tutoring classes, and also spend weekends and holidays studying for the many exams they must sit. There is fierce competition for the best schools and universities. Primary school is compulsory in North Korea. Top schools and universities are reserved for **Communist** Party officials and their families.

Festivals in South Korea

At Lunar New Year (*Sol*) in January, people return to their home districts to pay respect to their **ancestors**. Dressed in traditional costume, younger family members make a deep bow (*sebae*) to their parents and exchange formal greetings as a sign of obedience.

Korean Thanksgiving or Harvest Moon Festival (*Chusok*), around September, is South Korea's biggest holiday. Families travel home to offers prayers to ancestors, visit graves, bring treats to neighbours and view the full moon.

South Korea lights up at Buddha's Birthday, which falls during May. People hang coloured lanterns with paper prayers in temples to bring grace to the family. The beautiful Tobongsan monastery, near Seoul, holds prayers at dusk when the lanterns are lit. Lantern street parades are also held.

Huge lanterns on display at the Lantern Festival (Buddha's Birthday) in South Korea.

TRADITIONS and customs

The Wedding Duck

Wedding ducks are traditional tokens of everlasting love and good fortune given to the bride and groom. Each wooden duck is carved by a family friend, and brought to the ceremony wrapped in coloured cloths. The groom's mother throws the duck into the bride's apron. If she catches it, her firstborn will be a son; if she doesn't, it will be a girl. The wedding duck is kept on display at home.

The 80th birthday celebrations of Kim Il-sung. North Korean holiday celebrations feature massed singing and dancing, and parades of military equipment.

North Korean holidays

The birthdays of the former North Korean leader Kim Il-sung and his son, Kim Jong-il, are national holidays. They are celebrated with huge military parades and massed dancing, acrobatics and singing. Extra rations of sugar, sweets, dried fruit and meat used to be distributed as 'gifts from the Great Leader' on these occasions, but the economic crisis of the 1980s and 1990s put an end to this.

Since 1994, the traditional *Dangun* Festival (3 October) has been revived in the north. It celebrates the **mythic** founder of the Korean nation. Highlights include dancing and singing to North Korea's unique 'national music', folk games and tree planting.

The Five Fortunes

Traditionally, a man should possess the 'Five Fortunes'. These are wealth, health, no divorces in his family, a good wife and many sons. Only a man who has the Five Fortunes may be selected to carve the traditional wedding duck, and he must make only one in his lifetime.

COSTUME
and clothing

Hanbok

Hanbok (traditional costume) is a symbol of national pride in South Korea. Its design dates back 1000 years to the Goryeo **Dynasty**, when only the highly educated classes were allowed to wear it. Peasants by law could wear only white cotton or **hemp** clothing, earning them the title 'the white-clad people'.

A woman wearing *hanbok*, the Korean national dress.

Women's *hanbok* consists of a long, very full, wraparound high-waisted skirt called a *chima*, plus a short jacket (*jeogori*) tied at the front with a bow called an *otgoreum*. The bow, with its single loop and dangling ends, must be exactly right. Many layers of underclothes are worn to keep out the winter cold, including loose-fitting underpants, a full-length petticoat and wrap-around top.

Men wear baggy pants (*baji*) drawn tight at the ankles, plus a *jeogori* and long, loose coat (*durumagi*). The most distinctive feature of the men's costume is their black top hat made of horse skin. Traditionally, men wore their hair in a bun on the top of their heads, and the hat sat on top of this. Socks and shoes with turned-up toes are worn, and both men and women carry drawstring purses called *jumeoni*. These are decorated with elaborate knots and tassels that originally indicated the wearer's rank. Today, *hanbok* is worn for festivals and special occasions.

Colour coded

The colour of clothing was significant in Korean traditional dress. Unmarried girls wore yellow tops with red skirts; married women wore green jackets. On festival days, bright blues, reds and yellows were worn in imitation of court ladies. White is the traditional colour of mourning.

Day wear in North Korea

Plain, western-style clothing is worn in North Korea. Under Kim Il-sung, *hanbok* was banned and described as 'too backward', but now it is sometimes worn on special occasions. Mao suits (made popular by the **communist** leader of China, Mao Zedong) were once common but western-style suits (called *yangbok*) are now preferred. Uniforms are required wear for workers, university students and government officials.

Fashion in South Korea

In South Korea almost everyone wears western-style clothes, except on special occasions. At weddings, traditional *hanbok* is worn by the bride and groom for the ceremony, but the bride often changes into a white dress and veil afterwards. Simpler, modern versions of *hanbok* in cotton and hemp are becoming fashionable for everyday wear.

Elderly men wearing traditional dress at a Confucian ceremony in Seoul.

Icinoo

South Korea's best known fashion designer goes by the name of Icinoo. In 1997 she became the first Korean designer to show a collection in Paris. Her styles are known for their soft, feminine lines and fabrics, although she also designs smart, sleek business wear. Icinoo has been called the 'grand dame of Korean fashion'.

FOOD

A zest for spices

Traditional Korean food is hot and zesty, using spices such as chilli, pepper, garlic, ginger, sesame and mustard. Soy sauce, onion, leeks and soya bean paste (a strong, slightly bitter taste) add to the flavours. Steamed rice, soup and vegetables form the basis of all meals with side dishes of fish, pork, chicken or beef. Koreans eat lots of vegetables, including cabbage, green pepper, eggplant, pumpkin and cucumber. A full traditional Korean meal is called a *hanjoungshik*. It consists of grilled fish, steamed beef ribs, steamed rice, soup, vegetables and *kimchi*.

Famous dishes

Korea's best-known dish is *kimchi* – a pickled vegetable dish made of cabbage, leeks or cucumbers hotly spiced with pepper, garlic and chilli and left to mature in huge jars which are stored outside. *Kimjang* (*kimchi* making) is an important task for Korean housewives, who make enough in autumn to last through the winter.

Bulgogi (which means 'fire beef') is known as Korean barbecue in the west. Strips of meat are marinated (soaked) in soy sauce, garlic, sugar and sesame oil, and grilled at the table. Vegetables, chilli paste and lots of ginger are served with it. *Kujulpan* is a dish for special occasions. Pieces of cooked meat and vegetables are arranged around a central stack of small pancakes, in which the food is wrapped.

Bulgogi, known as Korean barbecue in the west.

Housewives make the traditional pickled vegetable dish *kimchi*, which is known as 'the dish that burns twice' because of its spicy flavour.

Mealtimes

It is traditional for the family to sit on the floor around a low table at mealtimes. Soup and rice are served in individual bowls but all side dishes are shared. Chopsticks are always used but they are thinner than Chinese ones and made of metal, not wood. Barley tea is a common drink with meals.

Throughout Korea, the main meal is usually breakfast, consisting of steamed rice and soup, plus tofu (soybean curd) or fish, dried seaweed (*gim*) and *kimchi*. Nowadays, South Koreans often grab a coffee and toast before work in the western way.

Canine treats

Koreans are well known for eating dog. The tradition arose long ago when hunting horsemen roasted or stewed the flesh of their dogs in times of food shortages. Today, dog is enjoyed as a treat in North Korea but rarely in South Korea.

PERFORMING ARTS

Rich heritage

Wall paintings in the Tomb of the Dancers, painted around AD 100, show that Koreans have enjoyed song and dance since ancient times. This rich heritage of dance, music, puppetry and drama styles continues in South Korea, where western-style dance and music are also popular. In **communist** North Korea, most traditional performing arts are viewed as backward. The state criticises traditional music as 'impure and depressing'. It has invented its own 'national music', based on modified traditional instruments and songs with western music patterns and political themes.

Listening to South Korean pop music is illegal in North Korea. Acrobatics, however, are encouraged, and the P'yongyang Circus (a famous North Korean acrobatics troupe) offers spectacular athletic entertainment.

Traditional dance

Traditional Korean culture is famous for its great variety of dances. Courtly dances originated as royal entertainment. They are slow and stately with solemn music and sumptuous costumes in the royal colours of yellow, blue, white, red and black. One example is the Crane Dance, which mimics the graceful movements of two white herons.

Traditional dancers in South Korea.

Foot puppets

Puppetry is an ancient Korean art, and foot puppets are a unique form called *palt'al*. The performer wears a mask on one foot outstretched towards the audience. He works the puppet's arms with long rods, lying down behind a curtain. The stories are usually humorous folk tales.

Nong-ak, the unique farmers' drum dance, has been listed in South Korea as a Cultural Treasure.

By contrast, folk dances are for the common people. They are energetic, expressive and spontaneous. Among the most famous is the spectacular farmers' drum dance (*nong-ak*), in which men beat drums strapped around their necks while whirling and leaping. Long streamers attached to their hats are twirled around with great energy and skill in time with the drums. Like many folk dances, the *nong-ak* originated as a harvest celebration.

Another spectacle is the sword dance (*kommu*) in which women hold long swords in both hands and clash them together as they move. More graceful is the *kanggangsuwollae*, in which women hold hands and chant as they dance in a circle under a full moon. Traditional dances like these are still very popular in South Korea.

Since ancient times, Koreans have turned to shamans (spirit guides) to help in times of trouble. The shamans' sacred dances are still performed today in South Korea. In the *kut* ritual to drive away evil spirits, the shaman hops and twirls with arms outspread, slowly building up speed until she reaches a trance-like state. Mask dances are comic affairs in which court life and wicked monks are made fun of. Striking masks express the characters of the dancers. At the end, the audience joins in amid much laughter.

'Flower of Korea'

Choe Sung-hee (1911–1967) took up dance when she was 15 and went on to become Korea's most famous dancer. In 1927, her ballet solo 'Serenade' performed in Seoul made her an overnight sensation. She became known as the 'Flower of Korea' and one of the top ten dancers in the world. In 1946, supporting the ideals of communism, she moved to North Korea where she continued her work in the Choe Sung-hee Dance Research Institute, preserving traditional dances. Tragically, she was executed by the North Korean government in 1967 as a **traitor**. The South Korean government could not forgive her for moving to the north and for years it was illegal even to mention her name in South Korea. However, after her unjust execution, her reputation was restored. Today, she is known as the person who saved Korean traditional dance for future generations.

Traditional music

Two traditional music styles exist in Korea. *Chongak* is court or classical music with a slow, sedate **tempo**. Instruments include the *kayagum*, a twelve-stringed **zither**, the *haegum*, a two-stringed violin and the *changgo* drum. Wooden flutes, gongs and cymbals also feature in traditional orchestras. Folk music, called *minsogak*, uses the same instruments but is much livelier and more expressive of emotion.

P'ansori is a music-drama performance with one singer/storyteller accompanied by a single drummer who makes comic remarks about the story being told. Performances last up to eight hours and tell folktales like the sad 'Tale of Simchong' ('The Blind Man's Daughter') in which a young girl sacrifices herself for her father. A further development of *p'ansori* is *ch'ang*. It has a large cast of singers taking different parts, plus an orchestra. In South Korea, the National Ch'ang Troupe, established in the early 1960s, carries on this tradition today.

Music in the family

Chung Kyung-wha is one of the world's finest violinists. With 32 recordings to her credit, she enjoys an international audience, and was awarded South Korea's highest honour, the Civil Merit Medal. Her younger brother, Chung Myung-whun is a world-famous pianist and conductor who was named **UNESCO**'s Man of the Year in 1995. He is currently South Korea's Honorary Cultural **Ambassador.** Another sister is also an accomplished musician and member of the acclaimed classical cello, violin and piano group, the Chung Trio.

The *haegum* is a vertical two-stringed violin.

Music in South Korea today

Many South Koreans have achieved international fame in western classical music. **Soprano** Kim Won-jung is an international singing star and has her own TV show. Choirs are very popular, and Korea won first prize at the World Chorus Competition in Vienna in 1997. The National Opera Group performs both western works and new Korean operas, and 31 symphony orchestras across the country draw large audiences.

The sweet, innocent image of the girl band Baby Vox is typical of female K-pop stars.

K-pop

South Korean pop music (also known as K-pop and locally called *gayo*) is all the rage in Asia. K-pop, like most Asian pop music, tends to be soft and sweet without the harsh rock sounds of western pop music, but rap is also very big. Many pop stars (*gasoos*) are former models, and white bleached hair for boys is 'in'.

Korea's most popular band until they split in 2001 was a group called HOT. One member, KangTa, is now a solo star with his own radio show. Baby Vox, a five-girl band, is also huge. Shin Hwa, a six-boy rap-pop band, has fans all over Asia.

LITERATURE

Ancient works

The earliest existing Korean book is *Samguk Sagi* (*Historical Record of the Three Kingdoms*), written in 1146 by historian Kim Pusik. *Samguk Yusa* (*Memories of the Three Kingdoms*) is a book of Korean **myths** and legends, written in the 1200s by the **Buddhist** priest Iryon. It includes the legend of how *Dangun* (half man, half sun-god) founded the Korean people. Both these classics record a golden age of Korean history from around AD 200–600 (the **Three Kingdoms period**) when the arts flourished. These works of literature were written in Chinese characters because Korean writing was not invented until the 1450s.

Korean classics

The first novel written in *Hangul*, the Korean language, was *The Story of Hong Kiltong* by Ho Kyun (1569–1618), in which a bandit hero founds an ideal, just society on Yul Island. Korea's most famous love story is *The Story of Ch'unhyang*, about a noble youth's tragic love for an entertainer's daughter and their struggles to be together. This folk tale was based on real people who lived during the Choson **Dynasty** (beginning 1392).

Eighty thousand wooden blocks were carved with type to print the book *Tripitaka Koreana*, one of Korea's most famous national treasures.

Tripitaka Koreana

The Koreans learned how to print books from the Chinese, who invented wooden carved block printing around AD 800. In 1237 a classic book of Buddhist thoughts and beliefs known as the *Tripitaka Koreana* was printed in Korea. The job took 15 years and used over 80 000 carved wooden plates.

Modern literature

In 1884, after years of isolation from the rest of the world, Korea opened its doors to foreign influences. New European ideas led to modern, realistic stories being written, the most famous of which is *Tears of Blood* (1906) by Yi Injik. *Peace Under Heaven* by Ch'ae Mansik (written in 1937) introduced Korea's most famous book character – the lovable rogue Master Yun.

The Korean War and **partition** of the country led writers from north and south to take different paths. North Korean writing is strictly controlled by the state, and most works are government-sponsored **propaganda**. The same was true in the south under General Park, although some fine books were written. The famous novel *The Land* (1970) by Pak Kyong-ri is a massive book about a landowning family and the clash of old and new cultures. This best-seller has been made into a TV series in South Korea. Today's most famous writer in South Korea is Yi Munyol, whose novel *Our Twisted Hero* (1987) won him the prestigious Yi Sang award. Set in a school, it exposes the danger of power and how it twists and manipulates people.

South Korea's most famous modern writer Yi Munyol (left), receiving an award for his books in 1999.

FILM
and television

North and South Korea's film and television industries are vastly different. The north controls all content and uses the media to reinforce **state** ideas. South Korea has a thriving independent film industry, helped by a law that requires at least 40 per cent of the movies shown in cinemas to be made by Koreans. TV programs are made on the western model and news is not restricted.

TV in North Korea

There is one state-run television channel in North Korea, which broadcasts for a few hours daily. Programs highlight state achievements – for example, the 'Dear Leader' Kim Jong-il touring industries or viewing military parades. Other programs celebrate how important workers are to North Korean society. They are portrayed as heroes, performing feats such as running with boulders strapped to their backs to build a dam. Indian-made (Bollywood) feature films provide entertainment. Very little information from the outside world reaches North Korea's citizens. **Censorship** means the state controls the news and only broadcasts positive stories about North Korea.

TV in South Korea

Four networks plus several cable channels offer a great variety of programs. Drama series are hugely popular, such as the top-rated soap opera called 'Endless Love' about two baby girls switched at birth. Soap stars attract crowds of fans at home as well as in Taiwan and Japan. Kung-fu action dramas like 'Flying Dragon' also rate well. After years of strict censorship in the 1960s and 1970s, under military dictator General Park, information is now freely broadcast.

Film

North Korean films are not shown outside the country so little is known about them. The state gives generous funds to **propaganda** films, which are made for political persuasion rather than entertainment. Storylines tend to support the government's views. Tales of heroic workers and the fight against the evil of western culture are common. It is believed that these films are technically well made.

South Korean film director Im Kwon Taek (centre) with actors Cho Seung Woo and Lee Hyo Jong.

The Father of New Korean Cinema

Director Im Kwon-taek (born 1936) is South Korea's most famous filmmaker. Since 1962, he has directed over 100 films, such as *Surrogate Woman* (1986) and the successful *Sopyonje* (1993). In 2002 Im Kwon-teak achieved international fame when his film *Chihwaseon* (*Strokes of Fire*), about the famous 19th-century painter Jang Seung-up, was awarded the prize for Best Director at Cannes.

South Korean films are currently gaining international attention. They tend to feature lots of action and brilliant special effects, although more complex plots are becoming popular. In 1999, director Song Il-gon's short film, *The Picnic*, won the Jury Prize at the famous Cannes International Film Festival. *Shiri* (1999), directed by Kang Je-gyu, is a classy spy thriller about a North Korean terrorist plot, starring Korea's highest-paid actor, Han Suk-gyu. *Shiri* broke box office records in South Korea.

Southern stars

South Korea's most famous actress is Kang Su-youn (born 1966). She won Best Actress in 1987 at the Venice Film Festival for her role in Im Kwon-teak's powerful drama *Surrogate Woman*. Ahn Sung-ki (born 1952) is a veteran actor of 53 films. He won his first international acting award in 1960 at the age of seven for his role in the film *The Teenagers' Rebellion*. His brilliant performance in the 2002 film *Chihwaseon*, about a famous Korean artist, helped win the film top prize at Cannes. Tall and handsome, Park Joong-hoon (born 1964) is one of the new generation of actors. He studied film in the USA and starred in many hits at home including a surreal suspense drama *Nowhere to Hide* (1999). He is now an international star and recently appeared in the 2002 Hollywood film *The Truth About Charlie*.

A film poster of the ground-breaking drama *Nowhere to Hide*, starring Park Joong-hoon.

ARTS AND CRAFTS

Arts and crafts in Korea were strongly influenced by neighbouring China and Japan. However, Korean artistic styles developed over time to be plainer and less luxurious than China's and more lively and informal than those of Japan.

Traditional painting

The Choson **Dynasty** (1392–1910) saw unique Korean styles of art emerge for the first time.

One of these styles was genre painting, which portrayed life-like, colourful crowd scenes from everyday life, in contrast to the more reflective Chinese

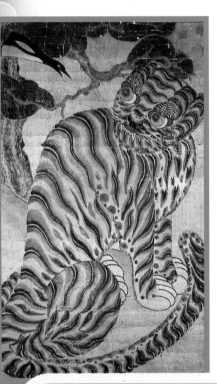

landscapes. Kim Hong-do (1745–1818) was the most famous of these genre painters. Another popular painting form was the 'Four Gracious Plants' style, focusing on plum blossom, orchids, bamboo and chrysanthemums, which were Confucian symbols of good fortune.

Korean traditional folk paintings (*minhwa*) are well known. Unlike other Korean classical artists, *minhwa* painters were untrained and did not sign their works. Techniques were simple and rough, and subjects were usually comical or light-hearted. Popular folk art themes were landscapes, hunting scenes, flowers and birds, and variations of the famous scene in which a tiger sits under a pine tree with a magpie in it.

Traditional folk painting (*minhwa*) featuring the popular tiger and magpie theme. The tiger is an important mythic beast in Korean folklore, usually represented as a friendly and kind guardian Earth spirit. The magpie represents good luck.

Folk-art sculptures

Throughout South Korea's countryside you will see simply carved granite stone figures guarding village and town gateways. These are spirit **totems**, placed to bring protection or good luck to the townspeople. Figures include smiling boys, animals, **Buddhist** symbols and pagodas. Wealthy travel agent Chun Shin-il began collecting stone folk sculptures 20 years ago to preserve them. In 2000, he opened Sejoong Stone Museum in Seoul, which houses over 10 000 examples of this ancient art form.

Minjung art

Art and politics mix in South Korea's *minjung misul* (political pop art). Painted on banners and posters during General Park Chung-hee's rule, *minjung* art displayed anti-government images in a simple, eye-catching way. But is it art? Experts now say yes, and in 2002 *minjung* art went on display at the Seoul Museum of Art. Exhibits include Hong Sung-dam's *Bath Tub – Mother I Can See the Blue Sea*, which portrays his torture at the hands of South Korea's military police by having his head held under water.

Western-style art

Foreign influences in the late 1800s led Korean artists to try European styles, including realistic portraits, **abstract** works and colour and shading rather than line. Jang Seung-up (1843–1897), known as Ohwon, was world famous for the beauty of his delicate paintings. His difficult life is dramatised in Im Kwon-taek's prize-winning film, *Chihwaseon*. Kim Whan-ki (1913–1974) pioneered modern abstract art in Korea. He founded the 'New Realism' movement, which blended an abstract style with traditional Korean subjects, as shown in his painting, *An Everlasting Song* (1957), with its images of mountains, birds and flowers arranged on a flat background.

Paik Nam-june (born 1932) is regarded as one the world's greatest living artists. He shocked local taste with early works such as *Klavier Integral* (c1960), in which a piano is decorated with '**found objects**' like barbed wire, toys, eggshells and a bra. In the 1980s he became famous for his television sculptures, such as *Video Fish* (1975) in which 54 television sets are arranged behind 54 fish tanks. Recent works include video animations, computer graphics and laser-beam displays, which aim to show the possibilities of modern multi-media as a form of art. Paik Nam-june was named Korean 'Artist of the Century' in 1999 and now lives in New York.

Modern art in North Korea

Strict rules are enforced as to what artists can paint in North Korea. Accepted subjects are war scenes, heroic workers and farmers, and portraits of the two Kims. North Korea's most successful artist is Kim Tong-hwan, who works in P'yongyang's Mansudae Art Studio. His paintings include the best-known portrait of Kim Jong-il. In 1998, Kim Tong-hwan was awarded the title 'Labour Hero', North Korea's highest honour.

Crafts

Over their 2000-year history, Korean artisans developed many skills in metalwork, jewellery making, granite stone sculpture, paper making, pottery and embroidery. However, war and Japanese invasion in the Choson period meant that most of these ancient skills were lost. After **partition** in 1953, South Koreans made a determined effort to rediscover traditional craft techniques. In North Korea, the government prides itself on its state collections of traditional handcrafts.

Decorative embroidery is used extensively for wall hangings as well as on traditional costumes. Selected designs have been named by the South Korean government 'Important Intangible Cultural Assets' – important cultural ideas like dances, designs or customs unique to Korea.

Beautiful examples of celadon (*cheong-ja*), with its distinctive soft green glaze, long regarded as the finest pottery in the world.

Celadon – the pride of Korean art

Since around AD 900, Korean porcelain (known as celadon or green jade pottery) has been prized throughout Asia. Porcelain is a fine, lightweight, white china with a hard shiny surface called a glaze. It was invented by the Chinese around AD 600. Koreans improved it by creating a soft green glaze with a crazed crackle finish that gives a beautiful depth and polish to the pots. They made simple elegant shapes and inlaid the surface with patterns using a secret technique. Traditional decorations included dragons (for power), flowers (health) and the crane bird (long life). Magnificent celadon ware was made for use at court and in Buddhist temples during the Koryo Dynasty (918–1392), but, with the Mongol invasions around 1400, the skill was lost. Today, South Korean master potters have revived the art of making celadon, creating pieces almost as fine as the originals.

Pottery for the poor

With the turmoil of the Mongol invasion after 1400, a poorer, coarser grade of pottery called *bun-cheong* replaced the more luxurious celadon. *Bun-cheong* is light brown and white (not green), and roughly decorated with rope or flower patterns. The Japanese invaded Korea in 1592 and kidnapped most of the country's master potters and took them back to Japan to revive the porcelain industry there. After that, Korea lost its place as maker of the finest porcelain in Asia.

GLOSSARY

abstract   not easy to understand or not realistic

ambassador   person who represents his or her country overseas

ancestors   people from whom one is descended

animism   belief that elements of the natural world (e.g. the sun, rocks, water) have living spirits

Buddhist/Buddhism   having to do with Buddhism, or a person who follows the Buddhist religion. Buddhism is a belief system originating in India and now practised worldwide, though primarily in Asian countries and cultures. Buddhists follow the teachings of the Buddha and strive for a peaceful state called enlightenment.

censorship   act of preventing people from expressing their ideas or opinions

Christianity   the main religion in most western countries. Christians believe in one God and follow the teachings of Jesus Christ, which are written in a holy book called the Bible.

communist   belonging to the communist political party or run according to the ideas of communism. In communism, the government controls all property and industry, and provides each member of the community with food, housing, and jobs.

compulsory   required, usually by law

Confucianism   religion based on the ideas of the ancient Chinese wise man, Confucius

conscription   compulsory call-up into the armed forces

Demilitarised Zone (DMZ)   neutral territory between two enemy countries where no military activity may take place, often referring specifically to the area between North and South Korea

democracy   a system of government in which representatives are elected by the people

dictator   a single ruler with complete power over a country

dominated   having power over another person or group

Dynasty   a series of rulers belonging to the same family

endurance   ability to withstand pain, suffering or exhaustion

enlightenment   condition of spiritual peace and understanding. Enlightenment is the main goal of the Buddhist religion.

famine   desperate shortage of food; mass starvation

fetus   unborn child

found objects   materials used for artwork just as they were found by the artist, such as ordinary household objects or items salvaged from the rubbish

haiku   Japanese form of poetry consisting of a single short verse, usually about nature and/or emotions

hemp   plant whose fibres can be spun and woven into durable fabric

isolated   alone or cut off from others

Juche Idea   political and economic theory invented by Kim Il-sung, which dictates that North Korea must not rely on any other country for goods or services but must produce all its needs by itself

mythic/myths   from fantasy or myths, which are ancient stories that usually explain how aspects of the world (or the world itself) came to be

nomads   tribal people who roam from place to place without permanent dwellings

partition   separation into two countries

peninsula   thin strip of land projecting from the mainland

phonetic   spelled out using letters to represent the sounds of a spoken language

political prisoners   people imprisoned for their political beliefs

privileged   given special favours or luxuries

propaganda   promotion of a set of beliefs to the public

reconciliation   making peace between former enemies

rituals   traditional religious or spiritual ceremonies

scholar   highly educated person

shamanism   religion in which followers believe in a number of gods and rely on shamans (priests) to communicate with them

soprano   female singer who sings the highest parts

state   any organised political community with a common government

tempo   the beat in music

totems   carved images of sacred spirits

Three Kingdoms period   a period in Korean history from 57 BC to AD 668 during which three culturally similar kingdoms existed in the Korean peninsula: the Koguryo Kingdom in the north, and the Paekche and Shilla kingdoms in the south. This period was marked by strong Chinese influences and the introduction of Buddhism (in AD 372).

traitor   a person who betrays his or her country

UNESCO   United Nations Educational, Scientific and Cultural Organization; UNESCO belongs to the United Nations system. Its aim is to foster international cooperation in the areas of education, science, culture and communication.

USSR (United Soviet Socialist Republic)   the former Russian communist empire, also known as the Soviet Union, which included Russia and 14 other republics. The USSR split apart into separate nations in 1991.

yin* and *yang   opposite forces present in the universe, which people in many different Asian cultures believe must be in balance for harmony and good health

zither   stringed instrument played by plucking with the fingers

INDEX